TORTOISE BOY

OTHER PLAYS BY CHARLES TIDLER:

Blind Dancers
Straight Ahead
The Farewell Heart
I Could Sleep for a Thousand Years
The Butcher's Apron
Fabulous Yellow Roman Candle
The Sex Change Artist
The Art of Kindness
Café Voyeur
Red Mango, a blues
Rappaccini's Daughter
Cross This Bridge at a Walk

TORTOISE BOY
a chamber play

Charles Tidler

Copyright © 2008 Charles Tidler

Anvil Press Inc.
P.O. Box 3008, Main Post Office
Vancouver, B.C. V6B 3X5 CANADA
www.anvilpress.com

First Printing.

All rights reserved. No part of this book may be reproduced by any means without the prior written permission of the publisher, with the exception of brief passages in reviews. Any request for photocopying or other reprographic copying of any part of this book must be directed in writing to ACCESS: The Canadian Copyright Licensing Agency, One Yonge Street, Suite 800, Toronto, Ontario, Canada, M5E 1E5

All performing rights of this play are strictly reserved, and in all countries permission to perform or give readings whether by amateurs or professionals must be obtained in advance from the author: Charles Tidler, c/o Belfry Theatre, 1291 Gladstone Ave., Victoria, BC V8T 1G5, Canada.

Library and Archives Canada Cataloguing in Publication

Tidler, Charles
 Tortoise boy : a chamber play / Charles Tidler.

(Anvil performance series; 7)
ISBN 978-1-895636-95-6

I. Title. II. Series.

PS8589.I34T67 2008   C812'.54   C2008-904946-2

(Anvil Performance Series ISSN 1188-0872; no. 7)

Printed and bound in Canada
Cover design by Shawn Shepherd
Author portrait by Shawn Shepherd
Interior design & typesetting by HeimatHouse

Represented in Canada by the Literary Press Group
Distributed by the University of Toronto Press

The publisher gratefully acknowledges the financial assistance of the Canada Council for the Arts, the Book Publishing Industry Development Program (BPIDP), and the Province of British Columbia through the BC Arts Council and the Book Publishing Tax Credit.

"The tortoise is both black and bright."

—Herman Melville

ACKNOWLEDGEMENTS

The Canada Council for the Arts and The B.C. Arts Council for writing grants (2002); The Belfry Theatre and A.D. Roy Surette for an early workshop (2002); The Other Guys Theatre Company and director Ross Desprez for a premiere production in the Belfry Theatre Festival 04; The Banff playRites Colony, in partnership with The Canada Council, The Banff Centre for the Arts, and Alberta Theatre Projects, for a developmental workshop with dramaturge Bill Lane (2004); Playwrights Theatre Centre for a workshop and performance, New Play Festival (2005).

INTRODUCTION

Playwriting, says the teacher, is all about point of view. "Whose play is it?" we ask the playwright. "Whose story are you telling here?"

That formula is starting to sound pretty old and tired, now that we're standing at the great generational divide of the postmodern. At least in the mass media, it's become more than obvious that this is a time of multiple narrative and multi-viewpoint drama. Audiences seem more than capable of listening to more than one story at a time—and even giving ear to several voices simultaneously, especially when each tone of voice is vivid and distinct. In fact, if they don't see a bit of a kaleidoscope, they can start to get bored pretty quickly. At least in the world of television, if the producers don't deliver that montage, the viewers tend to produce it all by themselves, just by surfing channels.

And still, we teach our playwrights some strangely denatured version of the Aristotelian unities. We say you have to be able to walk before you can fly: one story at a time, a single point of view in each play. But maybe if you learn to walk too well, you'll never work up to anything more than a decent foxtrot.

Charles Tidler has taught playwriting to several generations of gifted students. I don't know whether he ever taught his students the lesson about point of view. But even if he did, he never learned to practice what he preached—and the result is a kind of playwriting which is pretty much unique in its challenges and rewards.

Rules are made to be broken, of course. And rumours of the rule-breakers have been reaching our shores for a while now. Somewhere else, authors like Sarah Kane and Heiner Müller and Charles Mee have been daring and delighting their audiences with plays that are really more like wonderful poems in desperate need of a theatrical arranger. But it takes a lot of courage to give up the orderly sequence of dialogue (he said/she said) in favour of this kind of dramatic text in the continual act of reinventing itself.

Of course, as Charles demonstrates so poignantly in this play, there's another huge reason why the playwright might choose to confront the challenge of multiple narratives. Each person's story is intertwined with each other person's life, and that's the wonderful truth of human existence. This is especially true in the lives of those who face an uncertain future each and every day. By setting these four interlocking stories alongside each other, Charles not only presents a poetic puzzle for his interpreters, but also conveys a vital truth about human community: no person lives alone, not really. Like the tortoise, each one of us carries our shell on our back, if we're brave enough to admit it. And each of us has lived at least one life story which is also a part of someone else's life. We need each other's story to make sense of our own.

That central image of the tortoise shell is, of course, the poetic evocation of the teenage boy's 'hoodie' which protects the back of his neck at all times. In the workshop production of the play which we presented at Playwrights' Theatre Centre in the spring of 2005, we decided that the iconic shape of the 'hoodie' could find a musical echo in the shape of the double bass. And somehow, out of this discovery came a live presentation in which a bass player must be one of the cast—with his huge tortoise shell that made beautiful (and awesome) music.

The element of live music was a persuasive reminder to the audience that these words could be savoured as poetry, whenever the dramatic shape might begin to seem elusive. In rehearsal, the presence of the bass player also helped the performers to abandon the constraints of naturalism, and to make the kind of improvisational leaps which seem to come so naturally to a jazz musician.

And that, of course, is another powerful metaphor articulated in this play. Life is improvisation, and *Tortoise Boy* is the blueprint for a theatrical event which can convey that huge, gentle truth.

—*Bill Lane.*
Toronto, August 2008.

CHARACTERS.

DICK, 50, a man.
(Also: Deejay; Charlie; Second Husband;
Jane's Dad; Store Detective; Tourist; Security Guard.)

SHERRY, 14, a teenager.
(Also: Tortoise Boy; Clifford Olson.)

JANE, 45, a woman.
(Also: Dick's Sister; Dick; Sherry's Mom.)

BEP, 21 in 1970, a nurse.
(Also: Dick's Mom; Hindu Goddess;
H.S. Teacher; Reeba.)

TIME.
The present (circa 1995); and the past.

PLACE.
A waiting room in the psychiatric ward
of a hospital; and other locations.

Tortoise Boy was first produced by the Other Guys Theatre Company from March 31 to April 11, 2004, in Festival 04 at the Belfry Theatre, Victoria, BC, with the following cast:

    DICK Mark Hellman
SHERRY Ming Hudson
    JANE Gina MacIntosh
     BEP Meghan Braem

Directed by   Ross Desprez
Composer: Tobin Stokes
Set Designer: Scott Powell
Lighting Designer: Shawn Derksen
Costume Designer: Erin Macklem
Stage Manager: Jen Braem

Tortoise Boy was presented in a workshop reading by the Banff playRites Colony on May 11, 2004, and again on May 20, 2004, at the Banff Centre for the Arts, Banff, Alberta, with the following cast:

    DICK Brian Dooley
SHERRY Alison Darcy
    JANE Catharine McNally
     BEP Elinor Holt

Directed by   Bill Lane

Tortoise Boy was performed in a staged reading by the Playwrights Theatre Centre on May 3, 2005, at the New Play Festival on Granville Island, Vancouver, BC, with the following cast:

    DICK Kurt Max Runte
SHERRY Anna Cummer
    JANE Patricia Drake
     BEP Suzie Payne

Directed by   Bill Lane
Musician: Paul Blaney
Stage Manager: Teresa Vandertuin

This book is for
Iz
and for
Juniper
xox

PROLOGUE

DICK
Once upon a while ago,
A boy of ten or so,
I know where a wild
Backyard pear tree grows.

Fluid as wildfire
October I run
Through the high dry grass
To leap the yellow sun

With glowing hands
And like a pirate claim
From the fruitful sky
A ripe and shapely flame.

The juices are forever sweet
As I land running on my feet.

SHERRY
I was like a tree.

JANE
Like a tree.

BEP
A tree with roots going down.

(*A small bell rings*)

JANE
Hello, hello—

DICK
Hello—

JANE
I was called—

DICK
I got a call—

BEP
Have a seat.

JANE
I understand my son—

DICK
Is my kid—

JANE
Is he all right?

DICK
Okay?

JANE
They said he, they, they said—

DICK
He cut his hand?

JANE
He's my baby.

DICK
I want to see my son.

BEP
You have to wait.

JANE
Observation?

PROLOGUE

DICK
Sedation?

JANE
What kind of medication?

DICK
Drugs?

JANE
Psychotic episode?

DICK
Withdrawal from reality?

JANE
What are you doing here?

DICK
What are you doing here?

JANE
Grow up.

DICK
Shut up.

BEP
Have a seat.

JANE
And what are you doing here?

SHERRY
This is my house.

(*Lights*)

SCENE ONE. DICK

SHERRY
I was like a tree.

JANE
Like a tree.

BEP
A tree with roots going down.

DICK
Word for word. Leaf for leaf . . . I build up a burnpile of brush and cut bush, rotten wood and dried refuse, roots, scraps, waste, green branches, anything cut down to the ground, dug out by the roots, empty feedbags, old stuff, yellow newspapers, anything that burns. Strike a kitchen match, and a quick lick of blue flame spreads smoky fire sweating up the green branches. A bouquet of gray boils and snaps, and the yellow centre collapses into orange noise. A fireball like a giant beehive explodes, and the bonfire eats, cracks, spits, speaks, and like you, like me, burns from the inside out.

Once upon a time, I built a cabin in the woods.

JANE
You did?

DICK
Yes. You know that.

JANE
All by yourself . . . no help from anyone?

DICK
I come upon a bear in the clearing, going through the compost bin beside the garden gate. He's eating eggshells laced with coffee grounds. I see him, and my life goes straight up my spine. I raise my hands in the air above my head and

bring them together hard. There's a sharp clap like a fist of noise in the air, like a nest of wasps let loose, *clap clap clap.* Hey! Hey! The bear stops eating and looks at me. He stands up slowly on his hind feet and takes a good look. And now, thank god, he turns on all four legs and runs away. His big fat butt disappears into the thick bush. The next day I find bear shit, sloppy strings of black turds in a little pile in the middle of my road. It's the last sign of bear on the place, his way of saying goodbye.

JANE
There's the ugly truth that all my lovers, including two ex-husbands, were nothing but selfish, self-interested assholes. They call you up to vent ad nauseam the evil world conspiracy devoted to their frustration. But not one moment of concern r.e. your mental health or economic stamina. And their voices go like pickles to any news reflecting well of you. Fuck them, you say, and you mean it, but it goes down like bile.

DICK
Child-killer Clifford Olson kidnaps my wife and kid in front of the Black Creek store south of Campbell River on Vancouver Island a couple of days before his final arrest while drinking with two underage girls in a clearcut slash beside the highway near Tofino. My wife and I haven't spoken a word to each other for over a week, but we need flour and salt and nails. We need gas and oil and kerosene. We need chicken feed. We need to get the boy, who's having trouble adjusting to his new school, away from his only friend for a few hours, and on the way back from town, we stop in front of the gas pumps at the store. I leave the truck running with the key in the ignition and run in for mail or milk or tobacco. We have to get the boy to a ballgame. He's the shortstop, I'm the coach. I'm only going to be gone for a minute, and that's about what it takes to get whatever else it is that we need. I walk out of the store, and my fucking truck is gone. What the fuck, it's backing around in the Black Creek store's parking lot, a big man at the wheel, hanging half out of the still open driver's door. Hey, *clap!* The truck jerks to a stop. The swinging door slaps the man hard in the forehead. What the hell are you doing?

CLIFFORD OLSON (SHERRY)
You were blocking the gas pumps.

DICK
But he gets out. He walks away. My wife and kid hold onto each other, shaking, cowering in the cab, pathetic. She still won't talk to me. Two days later, Olson's picture is on the front page of the morning paper. There's a deep purple bruise on his forehead where the truck door hit.

Tell me. How far down the deep well of fear are you willing to go with a shovel in a dry season? Clods of dirt, small stones, insects that bite fall down the back of your shirt. Try turning around twenty feet down a hole not much bigger than you are. Rock, stone, hardpan, rock. How much water a family of three needs when you're standing at the bottom of your well with a dry shovel is one measure of fear.

The odds are that confronting the cruel world with a blunt refusal to remember is a good choice.

JANE
That was a long time ago.

DICK
The only water in the well are my tears.

(*Lights*)

SCENE TWO. JANE

JANE
The sweetest dream?

Walking in a green forest of filtered sunlight, my baby son in a packsack on my back, his head down on my shoulders, snuggling against my neck like a gentle burn. Climbing up the cliff-side rocks a step at a time through the trees, through small bushes, then rocks and moss, finally bare, naked rock. Climbing with arms and legs, the handholds becoming footholds, the jigsaw pieces of the blue lake shimmering below . . . and here begins the roar of the waterfall. A roar like a beehive between my ears. An eagle plummets, and the clouds tear like cotton cloth in its talons. The last rock. On top of the bluff. Holding the boy out into the open air, the sunshine flashes sharp as a knife, and he slips, a flickering flame, a feather of terror in the screaming mist. Did I drop him? Is this really a nightmare?

DICK
That was a long time ago.

JANE
The years when my teenager son is still healthy, sweet baby, sweet baby, I fight despair like shutting a door to weather and put on a white apron to prepare a holiday dinner for twenty people, roast turkey, all the trimmings, biscuits, pies, sweet potatoes, oyster dressing, gravy dark as forgetfulness, almost forgetting my second husband didn't love me anymore. The only word between us passes in the mousy squeak of the back door.

DICK
This guy is the real dick. (*Second Husband*) Going out.

JANE
Out to smoke his pot, cannabis sativa, drink his whisky, Jack Daniels, walking in the garden out of sight of the kitchen window.

Sometimes a cold wind moves through me like a ghost lobotomy, and it leaves me hollow as a forgotten promise, scooped out like a suddenly abandoned house, the shutters bang like fists, and no one is near enough to give one goddamn.

I would throw myself, the way salmon spawn, into the path of a bus to save a kid, my kid, any kid. Most people would. He, my second husband, would not. He pulls the car over to the side of the road and tells my son to get out, and when he gets out, just drives away. I grab the wheel.

Stop this car. Stop this car.

SECOND HUSBAND
We're gonna have a wreck.

JANE
I'll run us into a tree.

He stops the car. My son comes up, out of breath, holding his side, oddly round, small, misshapen, like a little mouse in the rearview mirror.

SECOND HUSBAND
Look at the little soldier.

JANE
Thank god you stopped, you son of a bitch. Look me in the eye. I dare you, you son of a bitch.

SECOND HUSBAND
Watch who you're calling a son of a bitch.

JANE
I open the door for my panting child. Get in, sweetheart.

Two weeks later, the son of a bitch comes into the electric kitchen, red-faced, sweating, not looking at me as I wipe my soapy hands at the sink. What's going on out there?

SCENE TWO

SECOND HUSBAND
You better have a look.

JANE
The back door bangs. I take the steps down two at a time. In a puddle of light at the foot of the double garage doors, there's a grayish figure like a large rug fallen from a clothesline after a beating. I hear a little cry, sweet, gentle, calling me.

SHERRY
Later that week, at the hospital, he tells me, Sherry, his only friend, that he said to her, his mum, (*Tortoise Boy*) Mom.

JANE
What happened?

SHERRY
He said, what do you think?

JANE
The back door bangs. His shadow crosses our backs like a metal bar.

SECOND HUSBAND
What did he say?

JANE
He says he's all right.

SECOND HUSBAND
There's a right way and a wrong way to do everything, and everybody knows this, even the people who do the wrong thing. I find myself constantly correcting the boy. Talk about obstinate. Talk about lip. Does he have parents? It's all I can do to put him one way or the other on the high road to the straight and narrow. No half measures. None.

SHERRY
Running down the path, trying to keep up with his thoughts, he carries all that guilt, the whole fam damily, like a fire

between his ears. The smell of gas on his hands and the sulfurous stench of memory caked beneath his fingernails, afraid to touch the world at any point, convinced that even his breath will stain like a spreading liquid, harsh trance of fire, yellow orange bore of spiraling tyranny to mock his pain, and the whole world blows up. Boom. Boom.

JANE
The mother of the boy is almost wholly broken, wanting and needing at any cost a moment's peace, a little rest, one fucking night's sleep for crying out loud, please, hitting the exit bar across the door of the police station with my fists, furious for an unconscious passage of time substituting for the dripping pain, the antisocial status quo, the everyday psychodrama, teeth cracking under pressure, pottery breaking, furniture upturning, mysteriously broken keepsakes, photographs cut in two, sleeves cut from shirts, missing cash, exploding lamps, bedclothes soaking wet, drugs, arson, shoplifting, police reports, court appearances, psychiatric assessments, freefalling through hell, one moment of memory loss, please, please.

BEP
Have a seat.

JANE
The emergency room at the hospital is unlike TV's rushing crush of dolly shots and last minute rewrites. Here in the real world, time slows like institutional paint dries. I sit with the feeble in wheelchairs, the mindless on drugs, and the corridors fill with sad, broken people hoisted atop shiny gurneys. Everybody is out of focus. Everyone has misplaced their script. Nobody's story is being told.

BEP
Follow me.

JANE
I follow the nurse to the other side of a white cotton screen, and here's my son sitting on the end of a hard bed. He

SCENE TWO

swings his legs, smiling and giggling and whistling like an eight-year-old held unbelieving on a chair outside the principal's office.

SHERRY
He says (*Tortoise Boy*) Hi, mom. I'm a tortoise now.

JANE
Why won't you hug me?

TORTOISE BOY
The shell's too thin.

JANE
Sweetheart.

TORTOISE BOY
I don't know how to pull my arms and legs in.

JANE
Well, so, two weeks later. We walk around the grounds of the, the mental hospital. We scramble down to the rocky beach.

(*Seagulls cry*)

I didn't wear the right shoes for this.

It's beautiful down here. Look, there's Mount Baker.

Do you come down here often? I would if I had a beach like this to come down to. I'd be down here all the time.

You should go for a walk now and then. Be good for you to come down here.

Maybe?

So, what did you do today?

TORTOISE BOY
I better go back up.

JANE
Okay.

The last time I see my second husband alive, he's peeking around a plastic curtain in the picture window of his pastel pink motel room. It's snowing. He's watching me scrape my windshield with a small screwdriver. A Phillips screwdriver.

And then the little slut comes up from behind to have a look, putting her arms around his waist, and I throw the screwdriver at the window.

(*Glass breaking*)

A slice of glass the size of a dinner plate slits his throat like a razor.

(*Lights*)

SCENE THREE. DICK

DICK
My first live theatre is a Punch & Judy puppet show with the best seat in the house at the back of mom's shopping cart. All the hitting and bopping and beating up back and forth, clubs upside the head, all the yelling and screaming, insults, humiliations, in public, in the light, making light of private violence and secret knowledge, shocks me. *Zap! Bop!* Like sticking my finger into an electric socket. I'm two years old, yeah, and forever after consciously an individual.

There's a photo of Jimmy and me on a pony in front of a house with fake red brick asphalt siding. I'm probably three or four, Jimmy's maybe two. The leather saddle is warm in the sun, and it creaks beneath me like an old boat on the water. I have to sit back, making room for Jimmy as mom lifts him up to sit in front.

DICK'S MOM (BEP)
Stop it.

(Laugh track)

DICK
He hit me first.

(Laugh track)

I get the cowboy hat. Jimmy gets the furry chaps. The little black and white pony smells like a dark barn with bales of pale green hay stacked up to the rafters, and as I close my eyes, I hear my grandpa milking his cows, *psst, psst, psst.*

MOM
Sit up. Open your eyes.

(Laugh track)

DICK
You don't have to slap me.

(*Laugh track*)

MOM
Sit up.

(*Laugh track*)

DICK
Vicks VapoRub. Does anybody even buy the stuff anymore? Here comes my mother running down the hallway between the bathroom and the living room. She wears a fluffy, quilted, synthetic, two-tone lavender-and-turquoise housecoat, a mask of cold cream and pink beanrows of plastic curler implants in her head. Oh, mom.

(*Laugh track*)

My mother's got a crush on Dean Martin and never misses his boring TV show. Jerry Lewis is the funny one, but Dean Martin and my mom have one big thing in common—glug, glug, glug.

MOM
You can shut up or go to bed.

(*Laugh track*)

DICK
Most people keep the garbage can, a toolbox, cleaning rags, Mr Clean and bottles of bleach and Windex under the kitchen sink. My mother kept her liquor bottles there. And one day after school, between the baby sitter driving off suddenly with her new french-kissing boyfriend and mom coming home from the assembly line, Jimmy and me show off the vodka and gin bottles to all the neighbourhood kids. And Mike Sowercroft, on a dare of a dime, takes a drink of gin or maybe just in his mouth, swishing it around his

cheeks and teeth and tongue, and turns around real fast and sprays everyone.

(*Laugh track*)

DICK'S SISTER (JANE)
Mike. Don't. I'm going to tell.

DICK
All the kids scream and run out of the house through the utility room back door. That night at the supper table, mom keeps sniffing the air like something dead, some kind of animal, is under the kitchen sink waiting to be found.

(*Laugh track*)

My tenth birthday. The only person home after school is my mom. She's all dressed up, going out somewhere later. My dad is out of town working on the railroad gang, and I don't know where my brother and sister are. My mom is smoking, holding her cigarette behind her, lighting ten candles on a double layer chocolate cake. The cake is half the size of the kitchen table.

MOM
Happy birthday to you, happy birthday to you, happy birthday, dear Dicky, happy birthday to you.

DICK
I blow out the candles. Mom and me eat some cake and ice cream. I open my presents, all new clothes for Easter Sunday and a book of Bible stories with coloured pictures. I wanted a ball glove. My mom picks up the book.

MOM
Let me read you the story about Moses in the bulrushes.

DICK
Don't read to me. I'm ten years old.

MOM
Okay.

DICK
She puts the book down on the kitchen table and walks into the living room.

MOM
Try on your new shirt.

DICK
I hear ice clinking against glass.

MOM
Here's my ride. You're going to Aunt Pat's. Happy birthday.

DICK
From the kitchen I hear the front door close, and I laugh outloud because I suddenly guess what my mom is trying to tell me: I'm an orphan from outer space.

(*Laugh track*)

(*Lights*)

SCENE FOUR. SHERRY

DICK
Helping her down from the fire escape, I take her hand, and it's like picking a stick up from the ground. What were you doing up there all alone on the roof? You don't even have a coat.

SHERRY
And she says could I use your phone?

She calls home, and her mother answers. She holds the phone away from her ear.

DICK
I go into the kitchen, buttering sourdough toast and spooning gobs of strawberry jam on top. Then I go back into the other room.

SHERRY
And she's talking in sharp, mousy whispers, saying she'll be home in a little bit and hangs up.

DICK
You want some toast and jam?

SHERRY
I'm not hungry.

DICK
Come on.

SHERRY
No.

DICK
Do you eat?

SHERRY
Yeah.

DICK
What do you eat?

SHERRY
Stuff.

DICK
Real food, not just candy and chips.

SHERRY
Yeah.

DICK
What?

SHERRY
Food is food. You're not my mother.

DICK
Do you eat bread, pasta, eggs, fresh fruit?

SHERRY
I like Subway sometimes.

DICK
You like their sandwiches?

SHERRY
Not really.

DICK
So, you just go there and hang out?

SHERRY
You make my head hurt.

SCENE FOUR

DICK
What food group is cigarettes?

SHERRY
Vegetable.

DICK
What's the problem, you don't want to go home?

SHERRY
Sing me any song you want to sing except the song I cannot hear.

DICK
Do you want to talk about it?

SHERRY
She says thanks for the phone and walks out into the hall.

DICK
The door to my apartment is still open. And this time she goes down the stairs.

SHERRY
I can speak. I know words. I know what language is. I have a vocabulary of tens of thousands of words. I know the importance of communication. I know how to make a sentence. But for me to communicate, to speak language, words in sentences, and for you to comprehend what I am saying, no, that's not going to happen.

Like I live in a distant future comic book, in a giant fishbowl city with streets in the sky and people with wings zip above skyscrapers, everybody looking up and pointing at pink and orange and peach explosions in the clouds, and a plague of mechanical insects blacken the whole earth, children naked and bleeding, crying in the alleys, beating off the eager rats with broken computer parts, plastic crumbling in the little kids' hands, but I leap up with a jet-pack on my back, going straight up to a domed rooftop patio where the rich and the famous and the beautiful clone happiness with the little blocks of video colours that crumble inside my brain until the dream is charcoal.

I won't look. Like when you're spying on people, you wish they'd smarten up, at least put on some clothes. I mean, it's really disgusting what people do in private, masturbating, squeezing pus from pimples, pissing and shitting, eating, throwing up, brushing teeth, flossing, looking into mirrors, like, forever. Don't you have a life? Here's one cinching a leather belt around his neck. Here's another swallowing a bottle of pills. Another falling down drunk. Here's a man beating a woman. And here's a woman staring vacantly into space. Yeah, space cadet.

JANE
What? What? Tell me, what? What's going on?

SHERRY
In her hand, is that a pair of socks, a phone, a smoke, a drink, a gun? Who cares?

JANE
Don't tell me it doesn't matter, everything matters. Everything you ever do matters. What?

SHERRY
We go up on the roof. The boys are playing with knives, throwing their pocket knives at the toes of their shoes.

Let me play, too. And I do, scaring them both to peeing their pants, I'm so good at throwing the knives at their toes. They chase me away, pushing me hard to the edge of the roof. I keep running away along the edge, and when I get to the fire escape landing, I jump, a little flip and grab the rail with my hands. I have to laugh, hearing those boys scream at the empty sky, thinking I jumped off the roof.

JANE
Where, where did he go?

SCENE FOUR

SHERRY
Sorry, I have to laugh, stupid boys.

JANE
Did he go home with you that night?

SHERRY
If you put your hands on your ears, I'll put my hands on my mouth.

JANE
You're telling me to shut up, okay, but you're here, and I'm here for the same reason. And that's all that matters. What?

SHERRY
Sing me any song you want.

JANE
If you hear anything.

SHERRY
Yeah, yeah.

Like when a house burns down, and the people who lived there sift through the smoky cinders, what are they looking for, the TV remote, the phone, a bottle of booze? Stupid people. There's a daddy named Dick and a mummy named Jane and a little boy they pick up at the nuthouse. But the mummy and the daddy don't look at each other. They never talk. The little boy doesn't even have a name. I call him Tortoise Boy because he lives inside his shell.

(*Glass breaking*)

His left fist strikes the window, glass flying, glass and blood mix in the air, his pinkie sliced like a pickle to the bone, and a voice from above and behind him, the voice of a friend, friendly and warm and concerned for his well-being, a friend steady as a rock, says you've put your left fist through the window, wrapping up the whole thing, the incident, with a rag of love. Why put your fist through a window? I say go ahead, but time and space and all the shit in the world won't give one good goddamn whether you do it or not.

Like a man died at the city pool today, and the lifeguard on duty tells everybody they have to get out, and we're like a bunch of pigeons roosting down in the ladies change room. All we can talk about, of course, is the drowned man who hit his head on the edge of the pool and drowned before anyone, himself included apparently, could do anything about it. Two girls say they've never seen a drowned man before. A woman about thirty says I've never seen a drowned man either, and I certainly never before swam in a pool when someone was drowning. One of the girls says yeah, that's weird, I don't know what to think about that.

BEP
I was swimming laps in the same lane with the drowned man before he drowned.

SHERRY
Did he look like Jesus?

BEP
No, he didn't look like Jesus.

SHERRY
But you were talking to the drowned man?

BEP
No, I wasn't talking to the drowned man. I was swimming in the same lane.

SHERRY
The same water?

BEP
Yes, the same water.

SCENE FOUR

SHERRY
Wow. You see?

BEP
No, I don't see. Because I'm here now, and the drowned man is the only one still allowed in the pool.

SHERRY
Like the time I see Jesus, there's this big bang so loud you wake up with your hands and your feet and your head sticking straight up in the air. You know, under the covers, you look like an upside-down turtle, and there's Jesus in the middle of the blue sky, walking across it like it's his front lawn. There's mashed potato clouds and little lambs with ribbons tied around their necks, and all kinds of fluffy shit floating by. And Jesus, like he picks up an axe and starts swinging it around and around overhead like a ferocious giant hummingbird. The blade of the axe is blood red with running fire. The sky goes inferno. The fluffy clouds blow away like cigarette ash, and the lambs stink like burning flesh. The axe melts like butter, the sky a halo of yellow rain. Ice cold rain floods the foot of the bed, and I wake up soaking wet. Whew.

(*Lights*)

SCENE FIVE. BEP

BEP
It was the way the intern looked at me eating a candy bar on my break outside the emergency room, his eyes like diamond drills boring into the depths of my soul, suddenly knowing everything about me: the eating of cakes, donuts, cookies on the drive into work, the washroom locked the first five minutes every day, and why the antiseptic hallway floods with new, fresh pine.

DEEJAY (DICK)
Next, the sports and weather, but first, someone on the line to play the game!

BEP
A typical mindless eating of time and consciousness, the guy on the radio is giving away stuff. A caller tells the deejay some big thing that happened in her past, and she wins a gift certificate for an all-you-can-eat cheesecake buffet. But the woman giggles, demurs, clams up, insists that her memory is blank, a blank wall, gyproc and tape, clear, clean, unremarkable, forgettable, no, nothing, that was a long time ago.

DEEJAY
Come on, come on, you're too young for Alzheimer's! There's gotta be one, big, cheesecake-important thing you remember, eh, the birth of your kids, graduation from high school—

BEP
No, nothing.

DEEJAY
Hey, hey, come on, there's a double chocolate cheesecake—

(*The line is dead*)

SCENE FIVE

BEP
The woman is me.

(*A small bell rings*)

I'm sorry, the doctor is unavailable. Have a seat.

DICK
You've got an American accent.

BEP
So?

DICK
Where did you go to college?

BEP
The Midwest.

DICK
Purdue?

BEP
Good guess.

DICK
So did I. What brought you to Canada?

BEP
Excuse me.

DICK
Say, did you know a guy at Purdue named Charlie Pipe?

BEP
No.

DICK
You were one of his girlfriends.

BEP
Have a seat.

(*A toilet flushes*)

Yes . . . I remember Charlie Pipe . . . twenty-five years ago, I was twenty-one, in town for less than two hours, getting up from the floor after making love on his rug, he tells me we're through, and although I've been seeing another guy, it hurts me deeply that this is how he wants the weekend to go.

So, why didn't you tell me this over the phone when I could still cancel my flight?

DICK
Charlie says (*Charlie*) I wanted to see you.

BEP
You wanted to fuck me.

CHARLIE
I wanted to make love to you.

BEP
Oh, fuck you.

CHARLIE
I love you.

BEP
Do you have anything to drink?

CHARLIE
What did you want to talk about?

BEP
Opening a can of frozen orange juice, I slice open my right thumb, the fat of it, two tear-shaped cuts jaggedly explode. Running to the bathroom, stanching the thumb with a wet washcloth, shit, no bandages, Band-Aids, nothing but toilet

SCENE FIVE

paper to wrap the thumb, holding it in place with a rubber band. I see myself in the mirror. Idiot. Idiot.

CHARLIE
Are you okay?

BEP
On the white tiles behind, a trail of wet rose petals has followed me to the sink.

I'm pregnant.

DICK
What are you going to do about that?

(*A toilet flushes*)

BEP
There were ten or twelve of us, young men and women, drinking and partying all afternoon down by the river, under the bridge outside of town. Later, we jump into a couple of cars and drive for an hour into the country, following the river valley to an old farmhouse where a novelist in his thirties lives alone with two dogs and a typewriter and not much else. We set up shop at the kitchen table, cases of beer, couple bottles of whisky, a sack of chips, carton of cigarettes. I go out and stand alone for a long time on the back porch, just looking into the acid blue of the long day. He brushes by me walking out into the yard where the grass is high with vigorous green, and the sunlight lights him like a match. I follow him like a rope is around my waist, through the orchard, crossing a small field of grain into an oak and maple woods, the bugs lazy in the heat, spider webs of rainbow and dust, and we make love on the naked ground.

I love you, Charlie.

CHARLIE
I love you, too.

BEP
Back in town that night, there's a house party down the street, but it's late, after midnight, and walking by I won't go in.

CHARLIE
Well, I want to.

BEP
Okay, go. I run down the dark sidewalk, crying so hard I run without looking into his roommate Bob. He grabs me by the shoulders and says are you okay? And he kisses me, and I kiss him, and he says let's go to the party. No, I don't want to. I just left.

CHARLIE
Stay away from her.

BEP
He hits Bob in the face with his fist.

Let go of me!

CHARLIE
You're coming with me.

BEP
Goddamn you.

(*Lights*)

SCENE SIX. DICK

DICK
The night Art Garfunkle accidentally bumps his forehead on the trunk lid of a Hertz rent-a-car in the parking lot at Indiana Beach and says fuck is the first evidence to me that celebrities live in the real world. The night Art Garfunkle accidentally bumps his forehead on a trunk lid and says fuck, I'm out of my mind for taking my little sister and her girlfriend to hear Simon and Garfunkle while my girlfriend, ex-girlfriend, is down in Brown County fucking her brains out. The night Art Garfunkle bumps his head and says fuck, I'm the only stranger in the hot and smelly standing-room-only crowd, talking to no one, passing through, squeezing by, standing around watching people dance and talk and drink and laugh and kiss, going out to the large enclosed porch overlooking the lake. People at tables. Strings of lights. Moonlight. The sounds of silence. What a joke. Drinking and driving, I've tried three times in the past week to kill myself, once walking away after flipping over in a corn field.

DICK'S SISTER (JANE)
Dicky.

DICK
Here are the two girls.

SISTER
We've been looking for you.

DICK
They want me to drive them home now.

I run out of gas late one night in early September out on Normandy Pike, coming home from a date with a girl I will never see again. Playing her like an acoustic guitar, playing each other like crickets crazy in high green corn, her smell all over me, and my fingers still curl to the shape of her breasts. Under a full moon sky, walking with an empty gas can the long asphalt road, corn fields, the faint glow of town, and the courthouse clock tower in the distance. Tomorrow morning, or the next day, I get swallowed for good into the dark whale of '60s America whole.

The night I was drunk and writing poems on the living room wall with a paintbrush and a can of black paint, loudly denouncing T.S. Eliot as a fascist traitor of American poetry, wasn't what ruined the party. For that, you have to go back to the innocent hours of the afternoon when Charlie Pipe was showing me and a couple of other guys all around a whole empty house he had just rented for the fall term, saying he was going to pay the rent by selling rat poison.

Charlie Pipe had the exclusive Indiana distributorship for this rat poison that claimed to be the best rat poison on the market, and yet it was absolutely safe around pets and kids because the special poison formula killed rats and only rats. In fact, according to Charlie Pipe, you could even eat the rat poison, and it wouldn't hurt you. The rat poison comes in an aerosol can, and Charlie Pipe squirts out a small stool of lime green foam like a soft ice cream curl onto a dinner plate. It looks like Crest toothpaste, except it hisses.

DICK (JANE)
I say prove it to me, Charlie, eat it.

CHARLIE
Charlie Pipe says you're kidding.

DICK (JANE)
The sole distributor in the state of Indiana, and you refuse to eat your own product?

CHARLIE
Charlie Pipe says I haven't got time for this shit. I have to get ready for the party.

DICK (JANE)
Oh, yeah.

SCENE SIX

DICK
We're all getting hungry, and Charlie Pipe pops half a dozen frozen chicken pot pies into the oven. The kitchen stove, except for the toilet and the bathtub, is the only piece of furniture in the whole house, so we're all standing around the kitchen drinking beer and talking about poetry and pussy, the usual. Charlie Pipe has to go take a leak, and while he's in the bathroom, I open the oven door and spray a green cone of rat poison foam on all six of the pies. The other guys start laughing their asses off. Charlie Pipe comes back and says what's so goddamn funny?

DICK (JANE)
Maybe you better check the pies.

DICK
Charlie Pipe opens the oven door, and a cube of black smoke escapes. I swear, a black cube.

DICK (JANE)
Like Vietnam, it's agent fucking orange.

DICK
We all stagger out of the house into the front yard, laughing so hard we can't stand up. Except for Charlie Pipe that is, who bursts into tears.

DICK (JANE)
Charlie, you got no sense of humour. It's fucking funny.

CHARLIE
Charlie Pipe says you don't know shit, Dick. Look. Charlie pulls a crumpled letter out of his pocket. Read it.

DICK (JANE)
"Greetings . . ." Fuck.

CHARLIE
Charlie Pipe bawls like a baby and says I just got drafted.

DICK (JANE)
"Your local board wishes you every success."

DICK

(*Lights a candle*)

Young guys, friends and family, come home from Vietnam with pieces missing, legs, arms, brains, ambitions. They jump into brand new cars, drive back and forth, here and there and nowhere, off the highway into trees. War flips you like flipping a spoon from a table, like a tornado takes away a town in a minute. The night Bobby Kennedy gets shot I shoot up Highway 401 to Toronto in a red Ford Mustang.

Go, go, go. I remember the smell of gas on my hands and a place to sleep for a couple of nights, sitting up alone all night writing poetry in Susie Passcott's apartment, burning all her candles, studying a roadmap, listening to the rain. Memory touches like weather, like darkness, like time, like love. And passes on.

(*Lights*)

SCENE SEVEN. BEP

BEP
The next day, or was it . . . I can't remember exactly, but after the operation, a woman dressed like a nurse poured the football-like remains into a large glass jar and set it down on the table right beside me. I couldn't look anywhere in the room without looking through that jar.

CHARLIE
Parked on the street, grinding my teeth, biting my flesh until the fingernails bleed. The kids on bicycles circle, yelling, laughing, and then one, later another, accidentally runs into the side of the car. The boys say fucker when I yell at them. Three hours, sitting, smoking, thinking. Shit. Life is shit. Across the street, yellow light spills from a small, frame house, and she steps out onto the little porch.

BEP
Charlie?

CHARLIE
The kids on bicycles rise like crows in their cries. She takes two steps and reaches out a hand for balance. The kids, like a pack of dogs, come closer, and I get out of the car.

Fuck off.

They scatter like a glass jar shatters across pavement.

BEP
Jesus christ.

CHARLIE
Hurry.

BEP
Give me a cigarette.

CHARLIE
Get in the car.

BEP
Fuck, it hurts to sit like a knife.

CHARLIE
Lock the door.

BEP
Okay.

CHARLIE
Fuck.

BEP
What?

CHARLIE
I don't know.

BEP
Give me a light.

CHARLIE
I could be anywhere else right now.

BEP
You alright?

CHARLIE
I could give up being human.

BEP
What are you talking about?

CHARLIE
I could be a monster.

SCENE SEVEN

BEP
What?

CHARLIE
We killed a child.

BEP
You expect me to say something?

CHARLIE
Forget it.

BEP
Let's get out of here.

CHARLIE
I feel awful.

BEP
Start the car.

CHARLIE
I'm so goddamn tired.

BEP
Drive away.

The best highway in the world, endless, unrolling, and inside the bubble of the car, the silence throbs like a thought balloon of pure lead. We drive a hundred miles. We have to stop somewhere.

CHARLIE
What was that?

BEP
Something dead, I guess.

CHARLIE
A bird maybe.

BEP
I can't stop bleeding.

(*Rolling thunder*)

Was it waking in the night, in the sick yellow glow of motel neon, in the night, the rain dark, thick, like blood, like dreaming, breathing, waking, swimming in the rain, in the fire, the blanket wet between my legs, breathing?

CHARLIE
I don't know.

BEP
There was something, not love but something more than the sour air in a small room, shared between us, breathing.

CHARLIE
I don't know.

BEP
In the small alien room, on the white square of kingsize bed, he was sitting on the edge, breathing. No, crying.

CHARLIE
I don't know.

BEP
Broken like a stick, broken like rain falling. Broken like a small bird in a dark fist, like a fetus choking on a knot of rain, a rope of blood closing tight like night, like rain, like sap.

CHARLIE
I thought you were the rain.

SCENE SEVEN

BEP
Go to sleep.

He sits there on the bed, crying through the transparency of his inadequate, sensitive nature, incapable of embracing the buoyant fact that there is life after death. We can get over this by forgetting it ever happened. Go to sleep now.

CHARLIE
Memory is a shell I carry on my back.

BEP
Did he say that? I can't remember. Yes, I can. This is somewhat cruel, but I remember his selfish indecision to hold me like a wounded bird in his hands. I wanted to suck on his breasts. I wanted to rouse him into song. But he didn't know how to begin to touch me, how to lift my legs or move my arms or wipe my tears or press my words like oil to his naked body. I remember passing a shapeless rose like a knife, like a sleepless night, like eight hours of bleeding on a toilet.

(*Rain on a roof*)

CHARLIE
What was that?

BEP
Something dead, I guess.

The dreaded clouds unbutton, and the moon glows like a pearl on fire from the inside out. Scoop out the day with a spoon-shaped tool. Cut my boyfriend down from the motel bathroom door. Flush the weekend down the shithole to hell.

(*A toilet flushes*)

(*Lights*)

SCENE EIGHT. JANE

JANE
A loose stack of photos . . . in the only order their random fate allows. Somebody's mother, or sister, who knows who, I sure don't, but somebody once upon a time picks up a camera and snap, here's the black-and-white print decades later, rescued from a corner of my father's attic, out of context, unremembered, in my hand. Here: three upright men in white shirts and dark suits, their faces as pale as the tombstone beside them. Here: two frowning women lost in the shadow of a barn while a little dog dances in the light. But these paper-thin representations of reality are meaningless unless I know something about who these people are. I bet every one of them is now dead in their grave. They'd be . . . a hundred years old?

(*A noise offstage*)

Dad?

Dad?

Dad. Is that you?

Dad.

DICK
He says (*Jane's dad*) What?

JANE
I've been calling you.

JANE'S DAD
Oh, yeah?

JANE
What are you doing?

SCENE EIGHT

DAD
Nothing.

JANE
You need me?

DAD
No, no.

JANE
Come here.

DAD
What?

JANE
Who's this guy?

DAD
No idea.

JANE
Come on, look: a young, handsome man with an ugly scar from ear to mouth, leaning against the polished fender of a 1930s car.

DAD
That's a Packard.

JANE
Okay, but what's the story? Is he related?

DAD
Couldn't tell you.

JANE
You don't know who he is?

DAD
Haven't a clue.

JANE
A young, handsome man with an ugly scar?

DAD
You said that.

JANE
Well, he's got to be somebody's uncle, somebody's cousin.

DAD
So?

JANE
What happened? Was he in a car accident? Commit a crime? Fight a war. Did he awake alone, in a hospital, in the middle of the night, from a coma, with the sour taste of death in his mouth?

DAD
I don't know what you're talking about.

JANE
Did anyone hold his hand?

DAD
Don't be weird. Good night.

JANE
Dad.

DAD
What?

JANE
Good night then.

My dad is always waiting. The strongest memory I have of him as a little kid is my dad waiting in his car for someone, usually me and my friends, whenever we needed a ride somewhere, just waiting in his car, smoking and waiting. Always. Waiting.

SCENE EIGHT

My dad makes a circle of worn grass in the backyard, a brown grass track oval. And like a pony in a carnival ride for little kids making his sad pony cycle, Dad walks the path every morning before dawn. He waves his hands back and forth in a rhythmic flitty fashion at the level of his shoulders, leaning first to the right and then to the left. He chants a short repetitive verse. A mantra. Dad has been to India six times. Six weeks ago, he struggled to unlock the front door, his hands shaking, and dropped the ring of keys like small bells at his feet, a little too anxious perhaps to put the door between him and the week in the hospital where he had surgery to remove a tumour. This afternoon I watch as a cat walks all the way around the circle of worn grass without once stepping out of bounds, one of the strangest things I ever see a cat do. Just being curious, I guess.

Dad.

DAD
What?

JANE
What are you doing?

DAD
Nothing.

JANE
Standing at a window, drinking and smoking, looking out at the rain, coughing, holding his breath, holding down the dry, harsh smoke, and the rain sings into the dark nests of backyards, a car engine runs somewhere, the rain writes on the window, words wet as dark grass, blindingly green. Drinking and smoking and waiting.

Dad?

DAD
Nothing.

JANE
Smile.

DAD
I don't want my picture taken.

JANE
Outside then, on your path.

DAD
No pictures.

HINDU GODDESS (BEP)
Accept being unimportant. Learn to sit. Learn to wait and expect nothing. The act of waiting, determining to wait, and to do nothing but wait. In that determination, waiting is enough for all and for anything.

JANE
I keep a diary during my dad's dying. A very punctual, very personal, day-by-day account of his blow-by-blow deterioration. A hearty, hale man slowly becomes a bag of skin and bones that's to be slid into an incinerator.

I sit up nights with him at his bedside, writing while he sleeps—tries to sleep. He awakes crying out in pain, and I hesitate for a moment to call for the nurse in order to finish my sentence. Without doubt, I now want him to die.

I want it to be soon, at the mercy of my grammar, my logic, my agenda, and for fuck's sake, my memory. I hold his hand.

(*Flashbulb*)

(*Lights*)

SCENE NINE. SHERRY

SHERRY
Like I wrote a story about a wad of gum stuck on the wall above the drinking fountain, and the Grade 9 English teacher, Misses Welches, gave me an A. So like I stuck the poem on the wall above the drinking fountain with a wad of gum holding it up, and everybody thought it was really funny, except Misses Welches of course. Fuck her. Sing me any song.

(*School bell rings*)

All the kids are standing out front of high school, and someone says something about someone being different, and that's when all the rough stuff starts. My books down in the mud, and I remember looking down at my homework so neat and tidy and so out of place in the mud and thinking nothing makes sense in the whole world. Like one day I do my homework and, smack, my face is in the mud.

Leave me alone. Fuck you, I need some room.

A scream from somewhere in the sky, but no Jesus this time. It's the flag at the top of the flagpole, cracking in the wind, and I fall. But how can I fall down when I'm already down in the mud? Nobody knows the answer. My head hits the pavement, and my eyes, wide open, watch it bounce.

Like my homework was a really cool report on the tortoise. Did you know that their eggs are round and white as ping pong balls? Round as the earth, and that's where they lay them, in holes they dig in the earth. And that's where they live, in their shells in their holes in the earth.

Sitting in the hallway, kids going by. The bell rings. Ring, ring, ring, laughing, it's pretty funny not being in the world anymore. Open your eyes, there it is. But not really. Because like you're not real. Except maybe you're like a dot. A dot floating around inside a giant balloon bubble of thinking machine.

BEP
The English teacher says (*H.S. Teacher*) Hello.

SHERRY
And the bubble says, you can't see me teacher.

TEACHER
Are you coming to class?

SHERRY
The bubble says, you look funny.

TEACHER
The class is beginning. We're going to begin. Well, you can just sit there then.

SHERRY
The bubble says, what did she want, another carrot up her ass? That's funny. Did she think I was in her world? Laughing so hard, harder, I have to lie down, flat facedown on the floor, pulling my arms and legs in, hiding like a tortoise, my whole shell shaking I'm laughing so hard.

TEACHER
Do you want help getting home?

SHERRY
The bubble says, what the hell is that?

BEP
H, o, m, e.

SHERRY
The bubble says, who are you, some fucking nightmare?

(*Lights*)

SCENE TEN. JANE

JANE
Torn like an angry root out of my apartment, I'm tossed among people who consider the human condition a great opportunity to screw one other.

STORE DETECTIVE (DICK)
Will you come with me, please.

JANE
The drunk driver who killed the man on the bicycle tells the judge that he's just an average guy. The woman denied a kidney transplant because there's no empty bed in the hospital tells the TV reporter that she's just a nobody.

DETECTIVE
Name?

JANE
The immense. Wearing. Pressure. The uncertainty in my life is driving me to the edge. The edge where a lot of worry gnaws at consciousness like a bear on my skull.

DETECTIVE
Middle initial?

JANE
I lack ambition, competitive edge, any and all quarrelsome, adversarial instincts.

DETECTIVE
Address?

JANE
Put it off. Have a cigarette. Fall into the fat froth of self-inflicted lethargy.

DETECTIVE
Telephone number?

JANE
Under the harsh light of scrutiny, I blink, pretend to wander and go blank like a screen.

DETECTIVE
Birth date?

JANE
A parade of insomniacs plod by single file. Each carries a monster on their back, a bellowing, foul-smelling memory, vicious and violent, that strikes with claws like chainsaws, lopping off the right arm of its host. Did that hurt? Poking at it. Did it?

DETECTIVE
Height?

JANE
A broken thumbnail bio is more than enough baggage. Life is short, and memory just fucks it up.

DETECTIVE
Weight?

JANE
History is tyranny. Memory is chains.

DETECTIVE
Hair colour?

JANE
A loser with dog poo on my shoes, on my hands, caked in the ends of my fingers, creeping up my arm like the gangrene shadow of an old house before night falls, rubbing it into my hair, the smell of death in my nose, in my mouth. The kiss. The bite. The word. The promise. It all tastes rotten.

SCENE TEN

DETECTIVE
Scars? Tattoos? Prosthetic devices?

JANE
Oh, goddamn, I am so sad to spend one more night alone.

HINDU GODDESS
The *Bhagavad Gita* encourages withdrawing the senses from the objects of sense, like a tortoise, his limbs from all sides, oh many-armed one, thus mentality is stabilized.

JANE
Why words at all? Why not silence?

GODDESS
Like a tortoise, pull your head and four legs into the house of your skin.

JANE
Roll into a ball. Play 'possum. Fold the umbrella. Fold your hands. Walk away. Wash your hands. Turn your cheek. Give in. Give up. Don't fight it. Bite your tongue. Swallow it. Pretend you didn't see what happened. Flight. Take the exit.

GODDESS
Every fall the trees throw their bare arms up in the air. Like the veins of a brain made out of the sky, they throw it all away.

JANE
The past falls away in large haphazard chunks, like cardboard boxes spilling from the back of an open truck. When I get to where I'm going will there be any boxes left? What will be their contents? I chose this?

GODDESS
A solid wall of water turns into light, into rock, into a tortoise on a rock in the sunlight, dreaming of water, and drinking.

JANE
Oh, let me sleep like an animal on the soft dark fruit rotting at the foot of the tree of forgetfulness.

GODDESS
The tortoise says: I am, I am.

SHERRY
I am inside my skin.

DETECTIVE
Sign where I've put the x.

JANE
Standing here in the grocery aisle at the spice counter, I slip a bottle of fake bacon bits into my purse. There's a rush like, like garbage draining.

DETECTIVE
And here.

JANE
Two inches tall, I walk past the girl at the cash register.

DETECTIVE
And here.

JANE
How many times do I have to sign my name?

DETECTIVE
Where I've put the x, please.

JANE
Okay.

DETECTIVE
We appreciate your cooperation.

SCENE TEN

JANE
Okay.

DETECTIVE
We're not going to prosecute, but you're barred from ever entering our premises again.

JANE
I understand. Thank you.

DETECTIVE
I'll escort you to the nearest exit.

JANE
I can do it on my own.

DETECTIVE
This way, please.

JANE
You remind me of someone.

DETECTIVE
No, you're mistaken.

JANE
Have you ever lost a child?

DETECTIVE
Good afternoon.

(*Lights*)

SCENE ELEVEN. SHERRY

SHERRY
Getting into the Legislature Building was a total fluke, but now I know how it's done, and you can do it, too. Like I was just hanging around on the steps of the Inner Harbour, and I hear a horse cop clop clop clopping round the corner. I don't have a busker's badge, fuck them, so I pick up my guitar and blanket, roll it all up, magic carpet, under my arm, just hanging, cool, and tough as fuck you. I cross with the walk light because like I don't want to get arrested now, do I? Hang in the front lawn, playing with the little kids running around the fountain. I like the rainbow bubbles water makes in sunlight, and the little kids laugh when I get all wet.

DICK
And some Japanese tourist says (*Tourist*) Will you, please, miss, take picture?

SHERRY
Oh, yeah, sure. Many smilings later, I walk up the front steps with the tourists, gray slabs of stone piled up into a fairy kingdom palace house. There's bars over the basement windows, and people in yellow light are in there staring at computers.

DICK
The fat fuck guard at the big front door says (*Security guard*) May I help you?

SHERRY
Just looking. I step into the powder blue hallway and lose myself, bumping elbows, in the stream of tourists thick as shitty, old salmon falling apart to lay their dirty eggs. Under the big blue dome, everybody looks up like ducks in the park. But it ain't Jesus up there on the wall, just naked native women loading furs on Captain Cook's boat. A loop of velvet rope guards a staircase, but nobody's looking at me, so I jump it, like one step, and I'm running down the stairs, but

SCENE ELEVEN

nobody chases me. In the basement, people in suits and briefcases brush past, and I follow them into a hallway smelling like burned tomato soup, into a dining room smack up into a table where the Premier unfolds a linen napkin that's white as new snow. He's right under my nose but doesn't even look at me. The Premier puts a silver soupspoon into his mouth. I don't even exist. But if I had a gun, the dickhead, fuckhead, shithead who cut my funding—

Let go of me, fucking fuckheads!

(*A siren crosses from left to right*)

(*Lights*)

SCENE TWELVE. DICK

DICK
Highway 19. Apparently someone has shit their pants, and the rest of us on the crowded bus strain to achieve the patience of Job. In the middle of the road ahead, a clown with a red nose and a crossing sign waves, and a scatter of school children race across. Sunlight blazes the quavering asphalt. Again the clown waves, and the bus huffs and gasps through the intersection. Finally, the bus station materializes like a sudden memory, and the driver releases the door, wheezing, to the heat of the afternoon. One step out of the shell of the bus, my son throws himself into my arms. We turn around and around and around.

JANE
She says well, someone, at least, is happy to see you.

DICK
That was a long time ago.

(*Lights*)

SCENE THIRTEEN. SHERRY

SHERRY
This is the family restaurant where I go with my mum for bad coffee and stale muffins whenever I get a pass to go for a walk from the nuthouse. No, I know, like it isn't a nuthouse, it's a hospital. The wingnut wing. No, it isn't. There's this woman here in the hospital, Reeba is her name, who likes to stand outside beneath the roof of the porch where she can smoke and look down at the hospital laundry carts full of green and white laundry bundles that are like giant marshmallows on wheels.

BEP
Reeba says (*Reeba*) The green ones are mint-flavoured.

SHERRY
Reeba is chain-smoking and crying.

REEBA
Mummy. Mummy.

SHERRY
Either her mother is late picking her up to go to a wedding, or her mother has been dead for forty years. It's hard to tell which story is true. But like one thing is for sure: Reeba's going nowhere tonight because Reeba has a full pack of cigarettes. She's going to smoke them, one at a time, out here on the porch. Until they're gone. Her mum will just have to wait. I tell my mum this story.

JANE
Mum says (*Sherry's Mom*) That's not a story. Why did you tell me that?

SHERRY
I better get back. I don't want to be late getting back.

(*Lights*)

SCENE FOURTEEN. JANE

(*A phone rings*)

JANE
Hello? Who is this?

SHERRY
He says (*Tortoise Boy*), Who do you think?

JANE
Oh, my god, my son calls from Vancouver. He's in a shelter. There's a phone in the hallway.

TORTOISE BOY
He says, can you hear it raining?

JANE
I thought it was the line. You know, white noise. But now that he explains it, I can hear the rain.

(*A hard rain is falling*)

It sounds like sound effects rain you'd hear listening to a TV in another room. But that's not the truth. That's not what's happening here. This is real life. My life.

TORTOISE BOY
He says, I got a bus ticket.

JANE
This is my son, his voice. His life. He's coming home. We're talking like two people talk across a table of rain.

(*Lights*)

SCENE FIFTEEN. BREATHE

SHERRY
He says (*Tortoise Boy*) Hi, mom. Hi, dad.

JANE
My sweet boy.

DICK
My boy. My sweet boy.

JANE
Go to sleep.

DICK
Sit still. Stop thinking.

JANE
Fight despair.

DICK
Sit still.

SHERRY
Sing.

JANE
Go to sleep.

DICK
Stop thinking.

SHERRY
Sing.

DICK
Sit still.

SHERRY
I won't listen.

JANE
Fight despair.

DICK
Try to sit still.

SHERRY
Sing any song you want to sing.

JANE
Why talk at all?

DICK
A phone.

JANE
Why not silence?

SHERRY
I can't hear you.

DICK
A smoke. A drink. A drink.

SHERRY
Sing.

JANE
You son of a bitch.

DICK
Shut up.

SHERRY
I won't hear you.

SCENE FIFTEEN

JANE
You son of a bitch.

DICK
Shut up.

SHERRY
Hi, Jane, you basket of razors. Hi, Dick, you airport departure.

JANE
Sweet boy, sweet boy.

DICK
Sweet boy, sweet boy.

SHERRY
You fucking bag of razors.

BEP
Breathe.

JANE
Sweep the shards and go to sleep.

DICK
Never break a window with your hand.

SHERRY
You fucking flight departure.

BEP
Breathe.

DICK
Try to sit still.

JANE
Fight despair like nailing a door shut.

BEP
Breathe.

JANE
Why talk at all?

DICK
Stop thinking. Shut up.

BEP
Learn to sit. Learn to wait.

SHERRY
Sing any song you want.

DICK
The empty house a mouldy loaf of rain.

SHERRY
Except the song I will not hear.

BEP
Learn to sit. Learn to listen.

JANE
I'm out of cigarettes.

DICK
A phone, a smoke, a drink.

BEP
Breathe. Breathe.

JANE
Breathe.

DICK
Breathe.

SCENE FIFTEEN

SHERRY
Breathe.

BEP
Learn to sit. Learn to wait. Learn to listen.

SHERRY
The tortoise says, I am.

JANE
I am.

ALL
I am inside my skin.

(*Lights*)

(*Curtain*)

CHARLES TIDLER is a poet, novelist, librettist, spoken jazz artist, radio dramatist and playwright. His writings have won Canada Council awards, BC Arts awards, a GG nomination in drama and a Chalmers outstanding play award. Previous publications by Anvil Press include the stage play, *Red Mango, a blues,* and the novel *Going to New Orleans.*

He has worked for a living as a farmer, railroader, factory worker, gardener, typesetter, editor and taught playwriting at U of Victoria, Vancouver Island U, Banff School of Fine Arts and The Belfry Theatre.

Charles grew up in Indiana and studied literature and philosophy with William Gass and Barriss Mills at Purdue University. A Vietnam War draft resister, he has lived on the west coast of Canada since 1969 and is the father of two grown sons. He makes his home in Victoria, BC.